DIE LEERE MITTE

Random Access Series

....
7 ½
....

BERLIN

INDEX

Cecil Touchon, *Prosaetere*, p.5
Tim Gaze, *Asemic: asemantic but not asemiotic*, p.25

DIE LEERE MITTE
Random Access Series 7½ Berlin, 2020.
Edited in Berlin by Horst Berger and Federico Federici.
home: https://leserpent.wordpress.com/category/dlm/
twitter: @LeereMitte
ISBN 9798682677832

Cecil Touchon
PROASETERE

The idea behind asemic writing is to create artworks that are based on the act of mark making similar to handwriting but without reference to semantic content or literary meaning. It could be called a form of literary abstraction or perhaps non-objective literature. Hence each 'asemic writer' has a unique way of writing or making marks. One's mark making may change by the day or even by the moment if the writer is sensitive to the changing twists and turns of the mind. Additionally, each mark making tool and each surface creates differences in the mark making process and can inspire the writer to work in a variety of ways determined by the tools and surfaces employed.

When we look at handwriting, even if we are unable to decipher it, we are getting some sort of visual content out of it from looking at the marks and rhythms or distributions of the markings on the page. We can get a feeling of order or discipline or perhaps a frenetic energy, or playful or sloppy or it might seem confused or muddled. You might say this is the body language of the handwriting beyond the message conveyed. This body language is the part that is of interest in these works and to asemic writers in general.

In the western part of the world writing tends to be left to right across a vertically oriented page often in a bound or book form. A reader is often presented with a book environment in which to experience a work that moves from page to page. But you could say that there is really only one continuous line distributed over many pages.

A film works in the same way moving from frame to frame, scene to scene to unfold a work and so does a musical composition moving from bar to bar, line to line, page to page. Normally, we think of a work of art such as a painting or a drawing as being its own singular environment enclosed by four corners. With asemic writing works there is the possibility to have the idea of an ongoing work that unfolds over many pages in a continuum.

This brings up the subject of time. In a visual work of art we assume that there is not a time element involved, that we see the whole thing all at once unlike a musical composition that we can only experience as it unfolds over time. But this is not true. When we look at a work of art we do take in the work as a totality however, our vision is confined to a focal point and peripheral vision. We can only really say that we have seen a thing when it is, firstly, in the tiny part of our vision which is fully focused and secondly, when our attention is on what our eyes are focused on. This takes a great deal of concentration. To see a painting - which might require a thousand focal moments - must happen over time. A painting is really experienced more by our peripheral vision - that is fuzzy and out of focus - than our focal point which is clear and crisp allowing us to see in fine detail.

Take this page as an example. If you sit back and look at the page in its totality you can see lines of letters and paragraphs and spaces. But in order to read it you must start at the top and move your focal point across the lines of words, look for phrases or word groupings, punctuation, etc. in order to grasp what is being read. Not only that, if your mind wanders, then you must start over at the point where you lost your attention. Visual works of art require the same effort.

Even when you study the lines of markings in this book you will notice that your focal point must move around the images to take them in even though the lines are only an inch or so wide. As a reader, we are accustomed to read words in straight lines with all of the characters being the same font and the same size. Every tiny change in the organization of a book means something such as paragraph breaks, capital letters, bold, italicized, or underlined words, chapter headings, footnotes, etc. and we are accustomed to these conventions. So, to 'read' the present text, the approach is somewhat different.

For instance, while each letter you are reading now is distinct, individual and the presentation highly organized, in many of these works by Cecil Touchon most of the marks overlap and intertwine and move across the page in a visual flow suggesting the interaction of multiple, simultaneous events . In this writing that you are now reading however, the physical printing on the page all but disappears so that the words, as you read them, are being converted into a communication in your mind of the ideas they represent. You could not really say that you care about the physically written words aside from grasping the message they contain. This is the same way that people used to look at paintings. They were not so interested in the physical surface and brush strokes of the painting as they were in the image emerging out of those strokes of, let's say, a portrait or a landscape or an apple. At some point, certain artists started to think of the painting not as a representation of something else outside of the painting but as its own unique and autonomous reality. This was the beginnings of what we now call abstract art.

In the same way, language as we use it, is representational, it represents things outside of itself such as thoughts or ideas or descriptions. You could say that this representationalism is its only actual function. These drawings however do not contain the same kind of representational information. These works, on the other hand, are only about themselves and what they are; a potentially unending chain of what could be called visual music. At the same time, they are not representing any particular music or intended to become notation for music but are based on the idea of musicality and spontaneous, unique relationships.

Touchon's ongoing interest is in how the eye moves around a work, at what speed, in what order and according to what stimulus. What gives it rest, what excites it? What brings clarity, what causes confusion? What triggers boredom or inspiration?

The object of these drawings or writings is in moving the focal point of the eye along during the reading through repetition and progression of marks, cadence, movement, etc. It is a form of 'listening with the eye'. Listening means to place one's attention on a thing being heard. Listening is a form of focused attention.

Even though we hear everything around us we can only actually fully listen to one thing at a time. When we hear things, we are often not attentive to the sounds and hence are not engaged in listening to most of the sounds around us. If you stop for a moment just now and listen carefully to the sounds around you, you will notice the sounds that you have been hearing but have not been listening to.

In the same way, we see whatever is around us but without our full focused attention we are not actively and attentively taking in what we see. The reader is encouraged to approach these works as one might listen to music. This might include numerous repeated readings or listenings studying how the work flows, how it shifts and turns and returns to certain themes or motifs or types of markings.

Compared to reading, the creation of the markings is a whole other story. In a certain way it is a process of performing with a pen in the way that a musician might perform with a musical instrument. However, instead of hearing the sounds of the piano or violin, one is observing the motions of the pen working its way across the page. As an observer during the process of making such works, Touchon's attention is on the state of consciousness that he is in at that moment and how that is expressed in the movements of the hand across a blank sheet of paper. It is something of a spiritual practice. He allows his intuition to work silently and unchecked within the boundaries of the process. He is exploring in an experimental way to see what happens under what conditions. It could be called a form of improvisational meditation.

Cecil Touchon

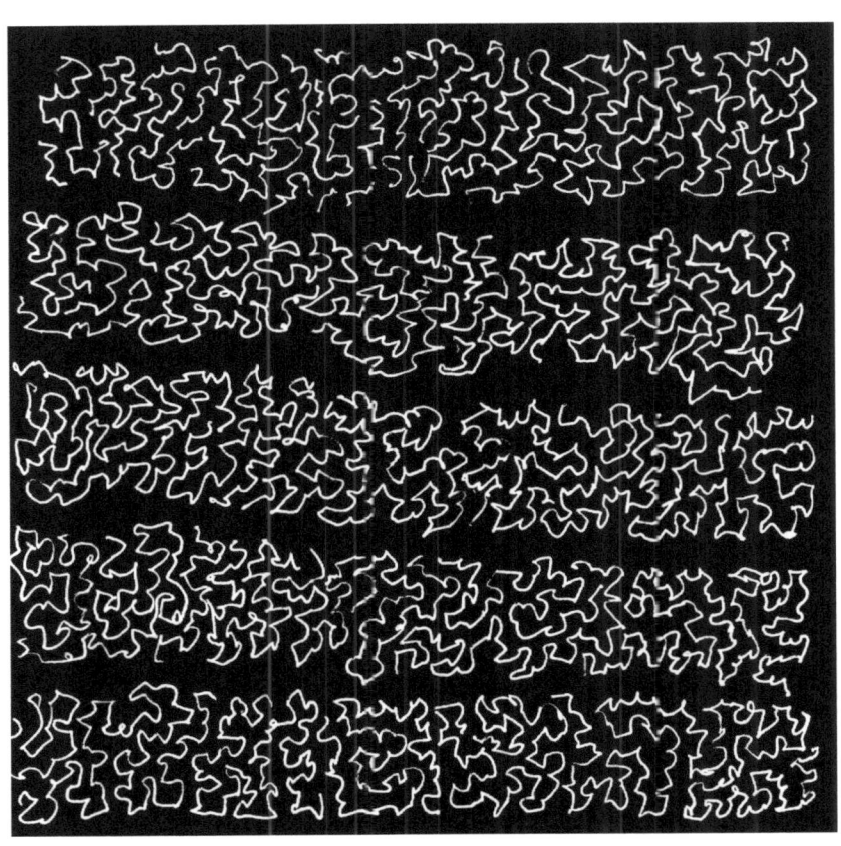

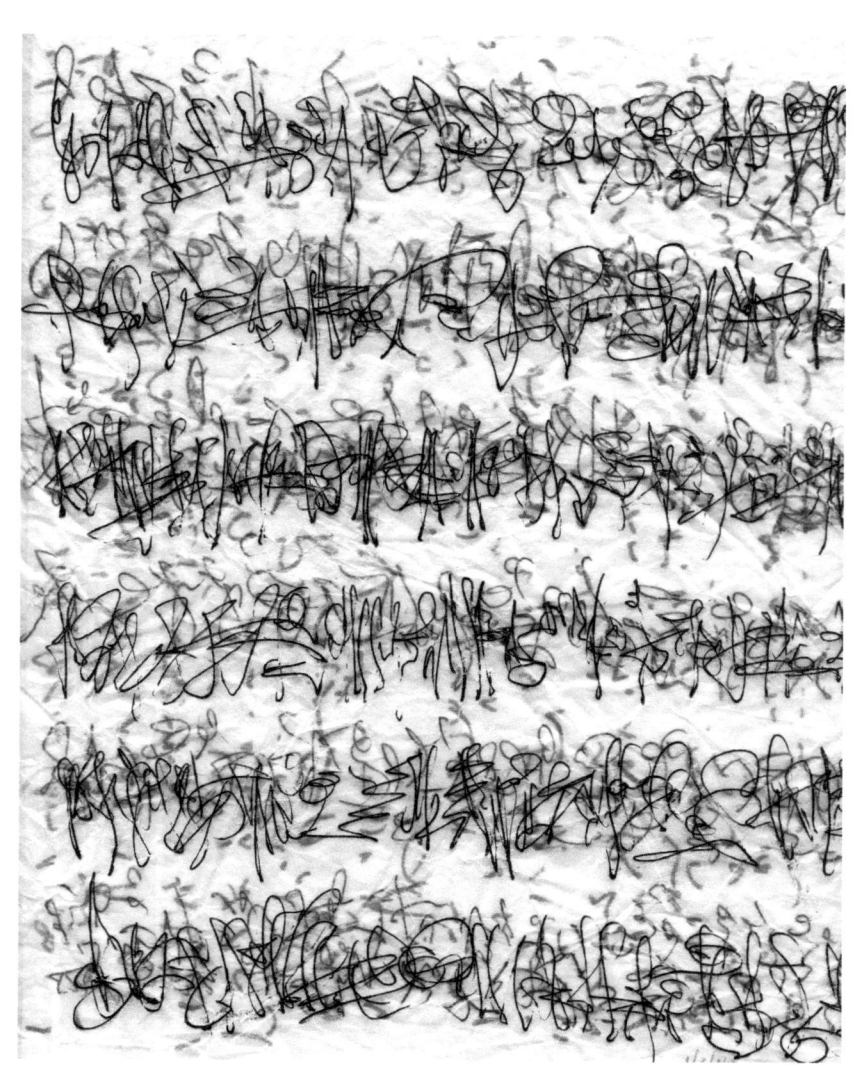

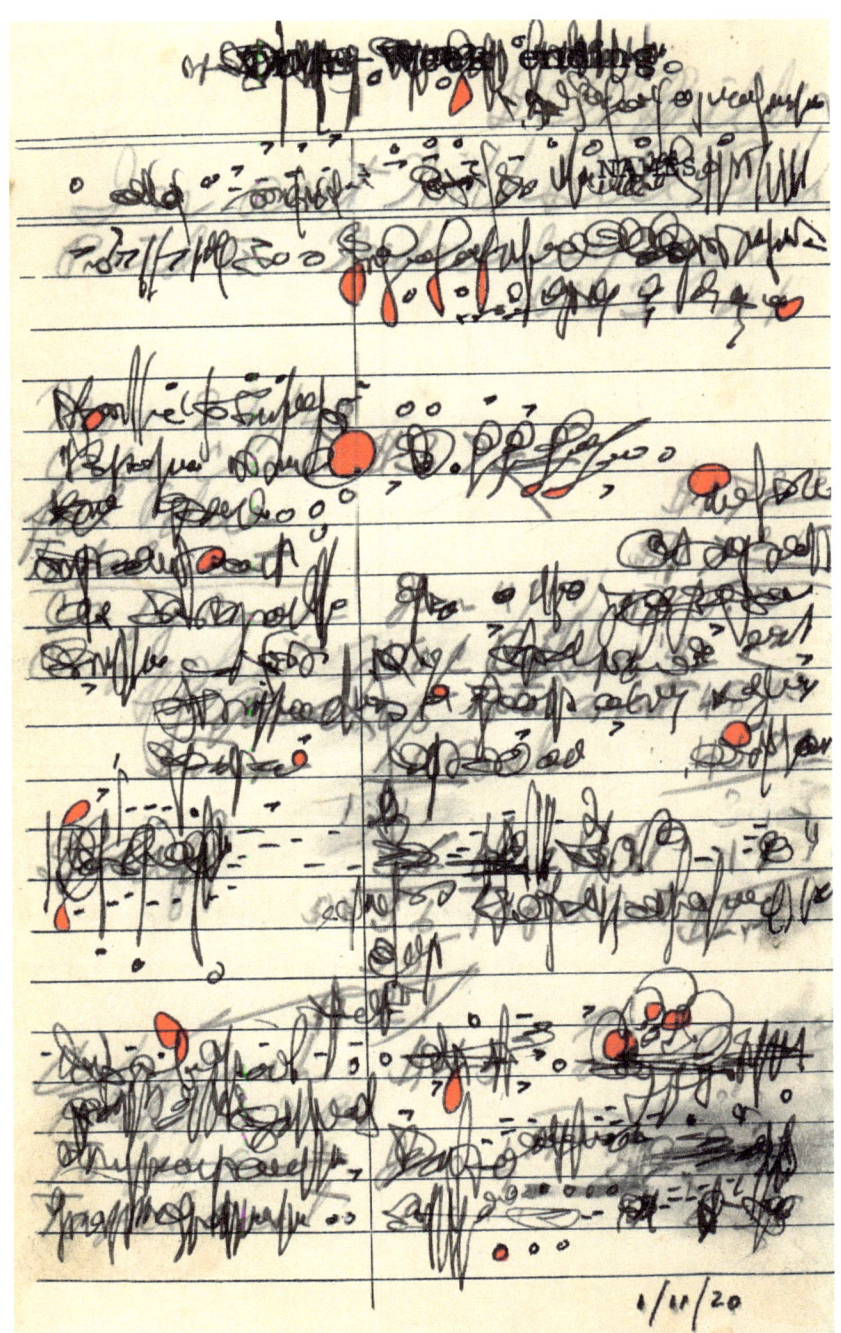

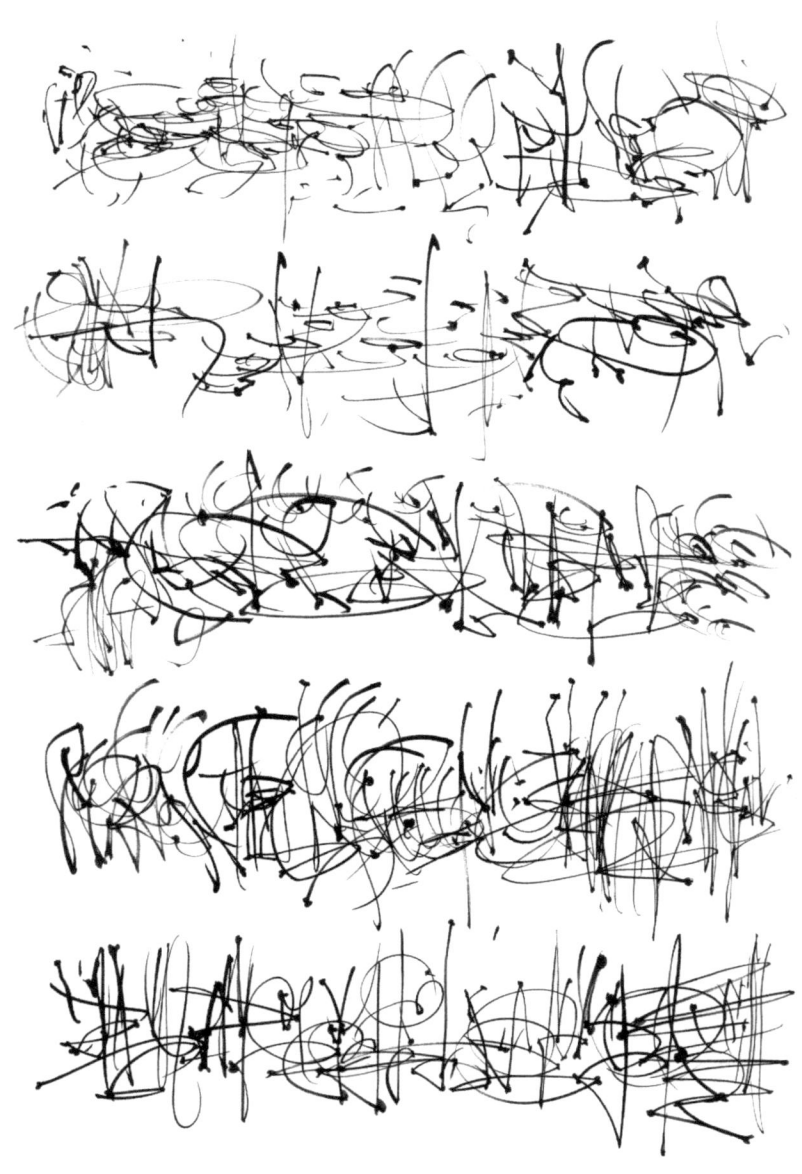

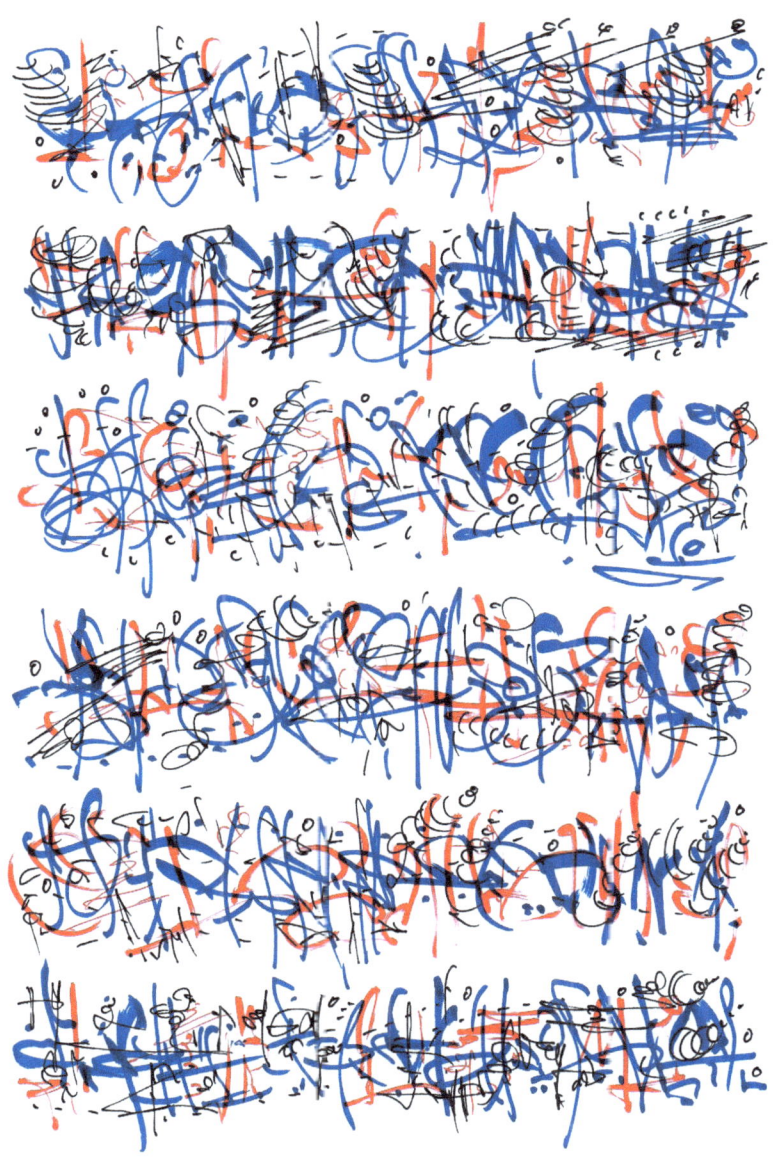

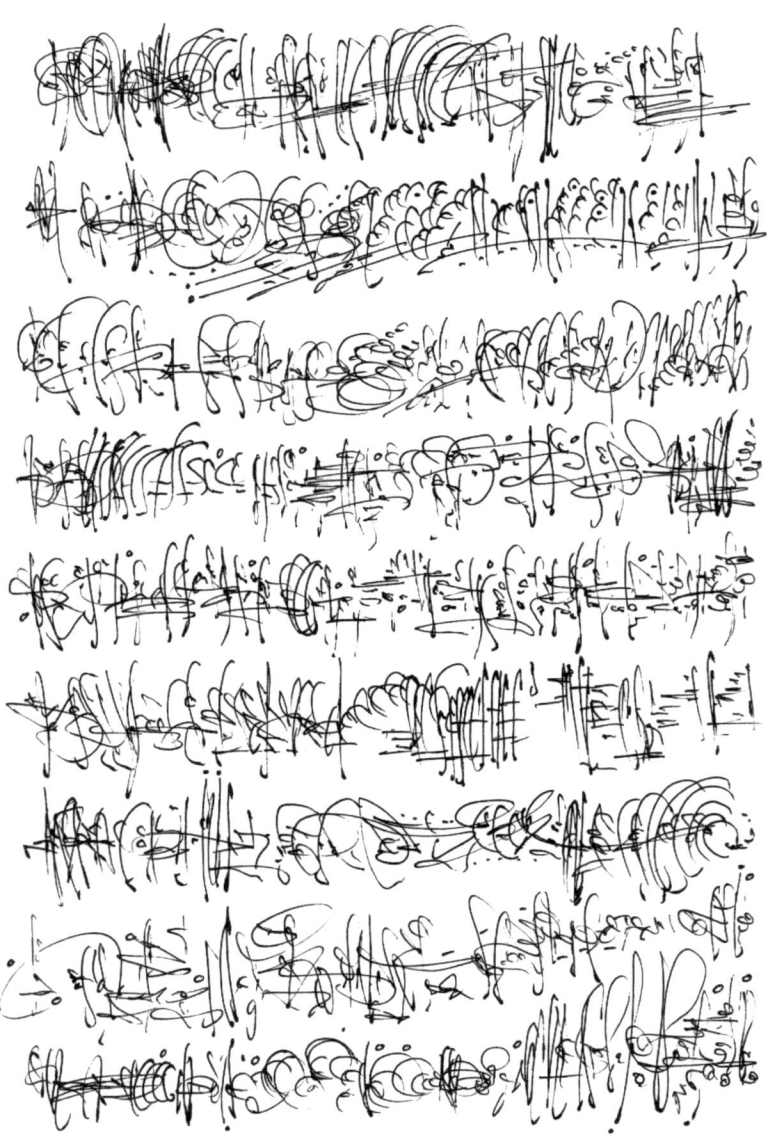

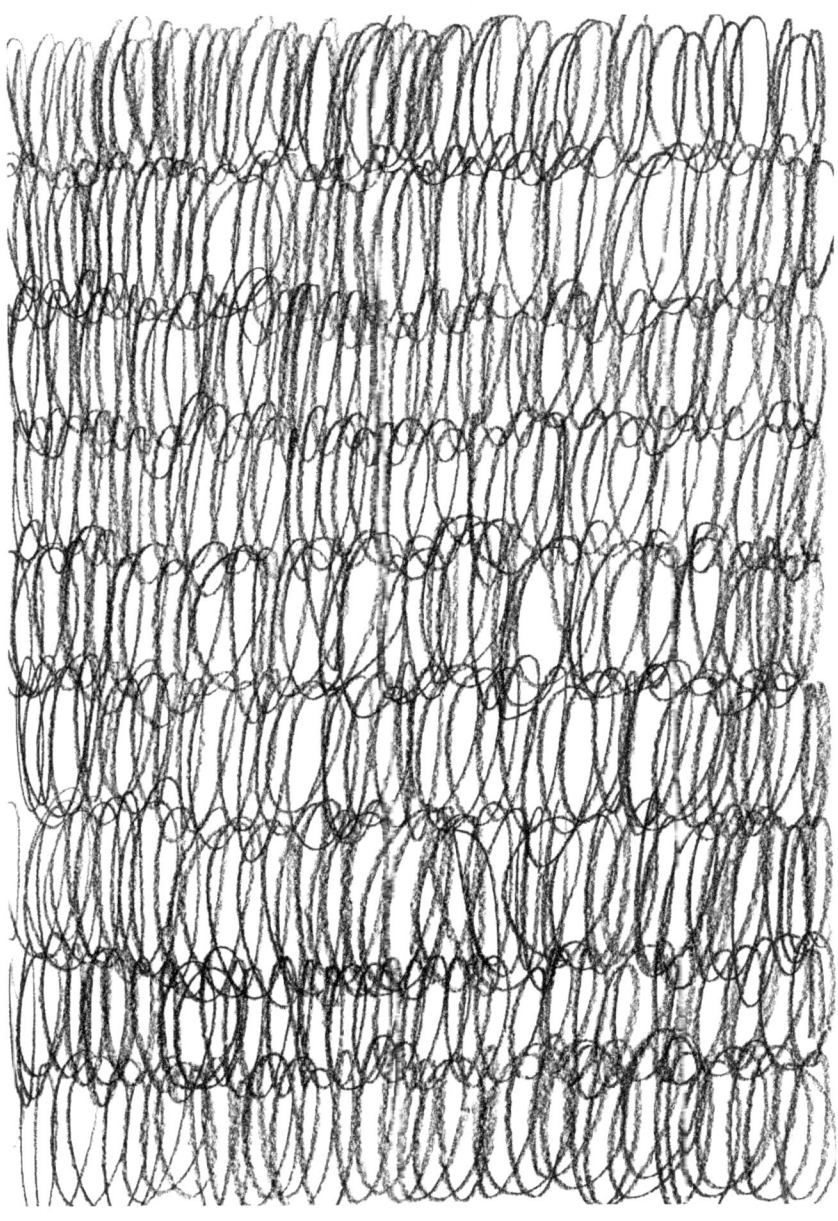

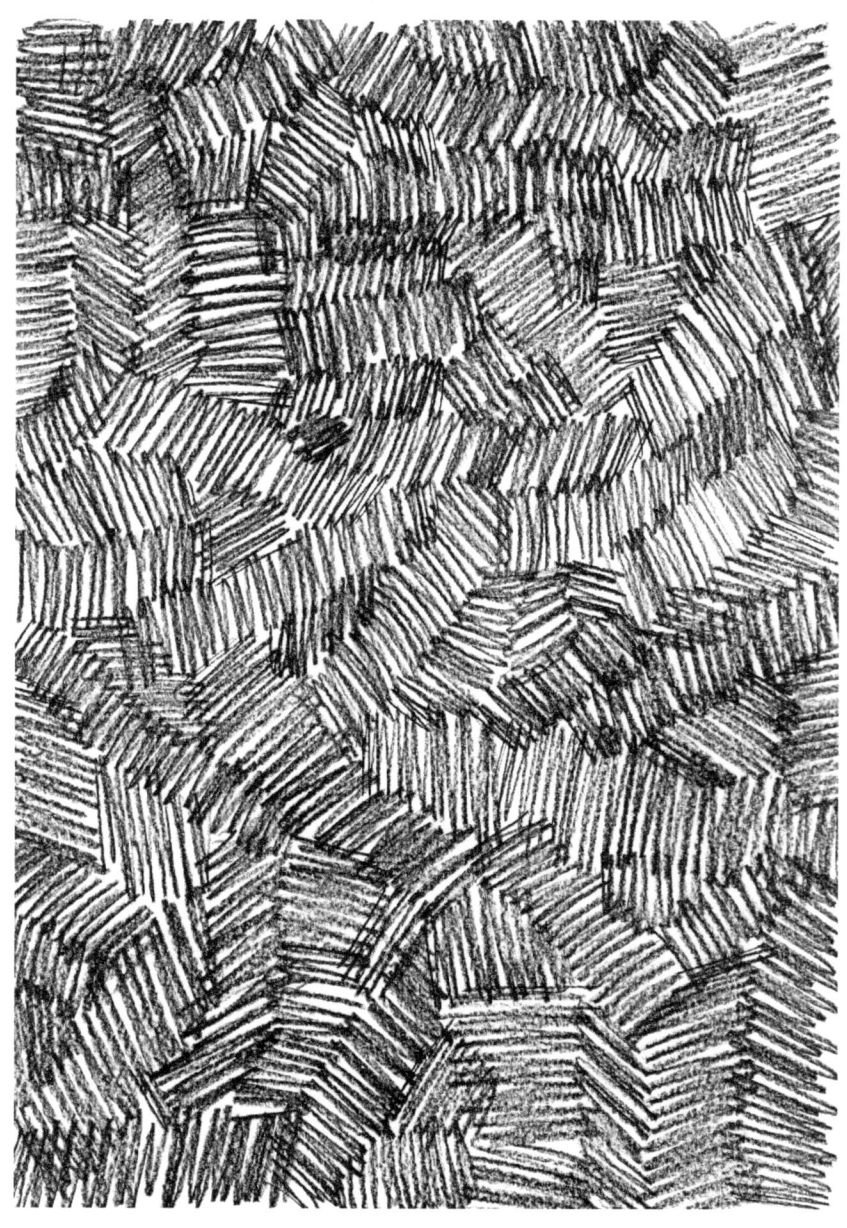

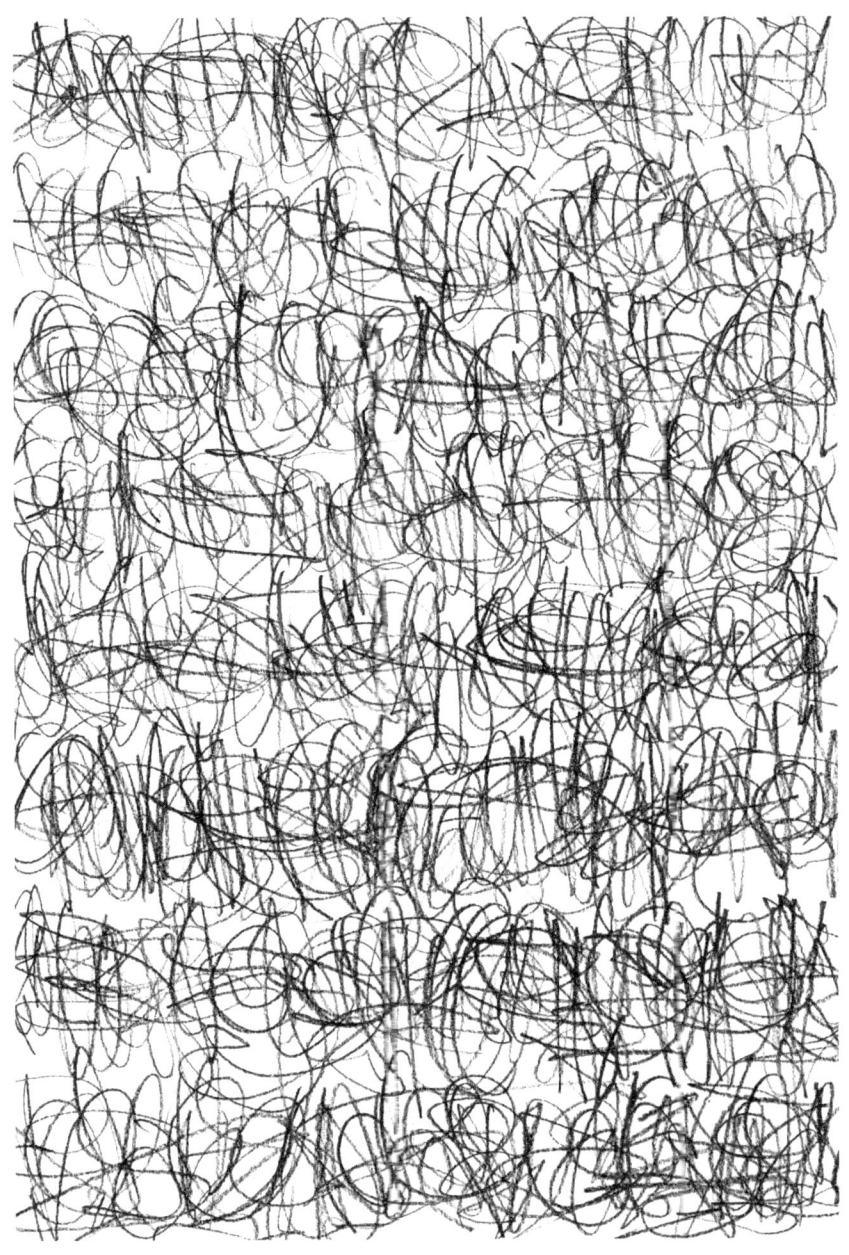

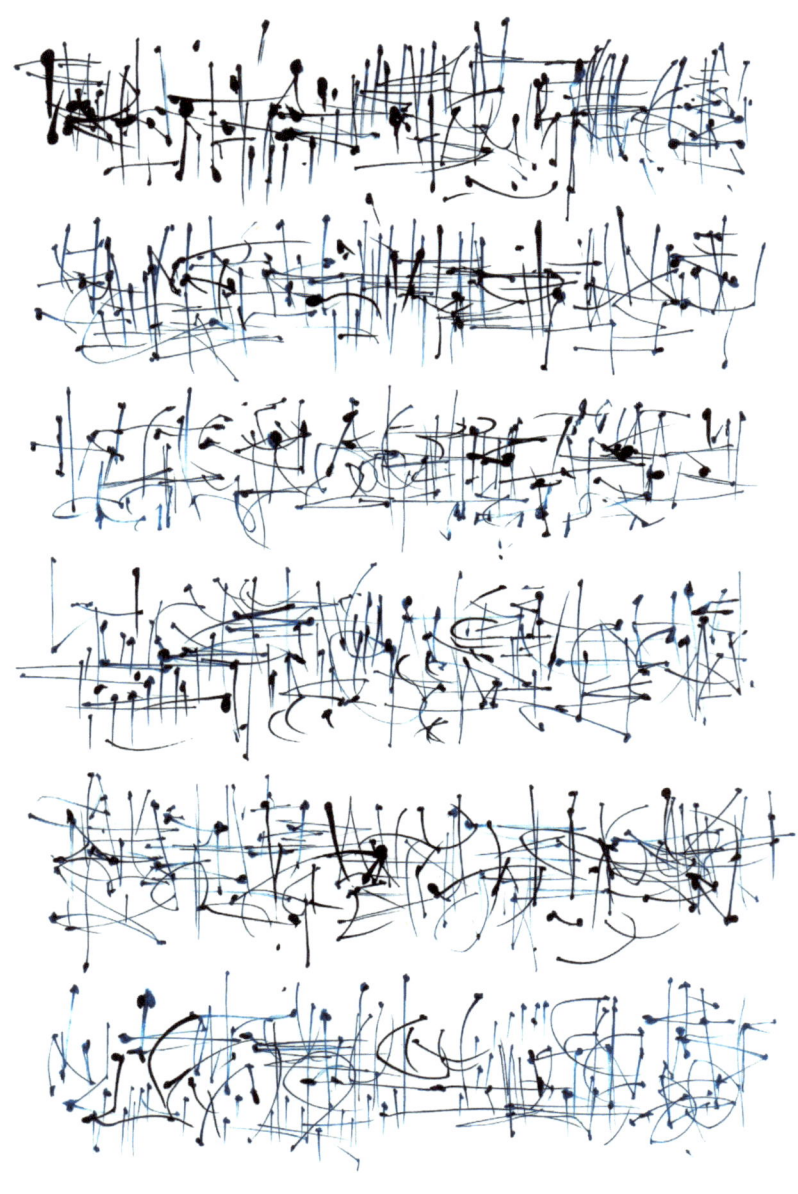

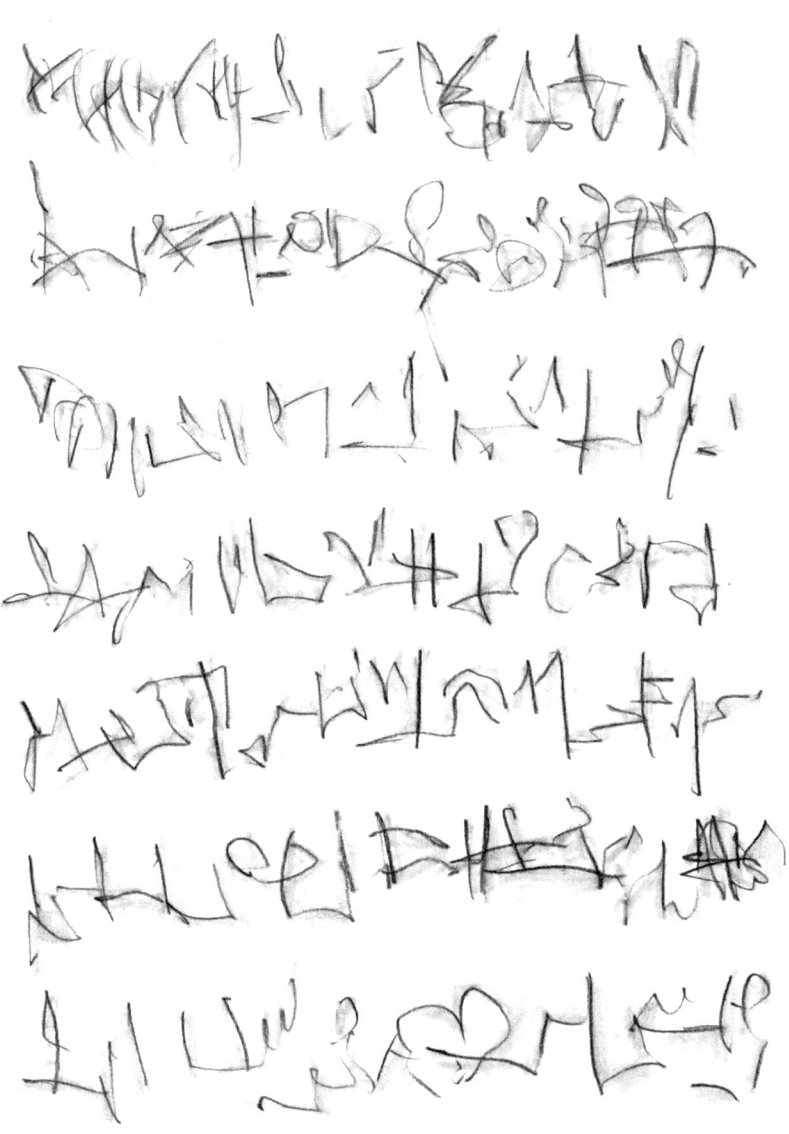

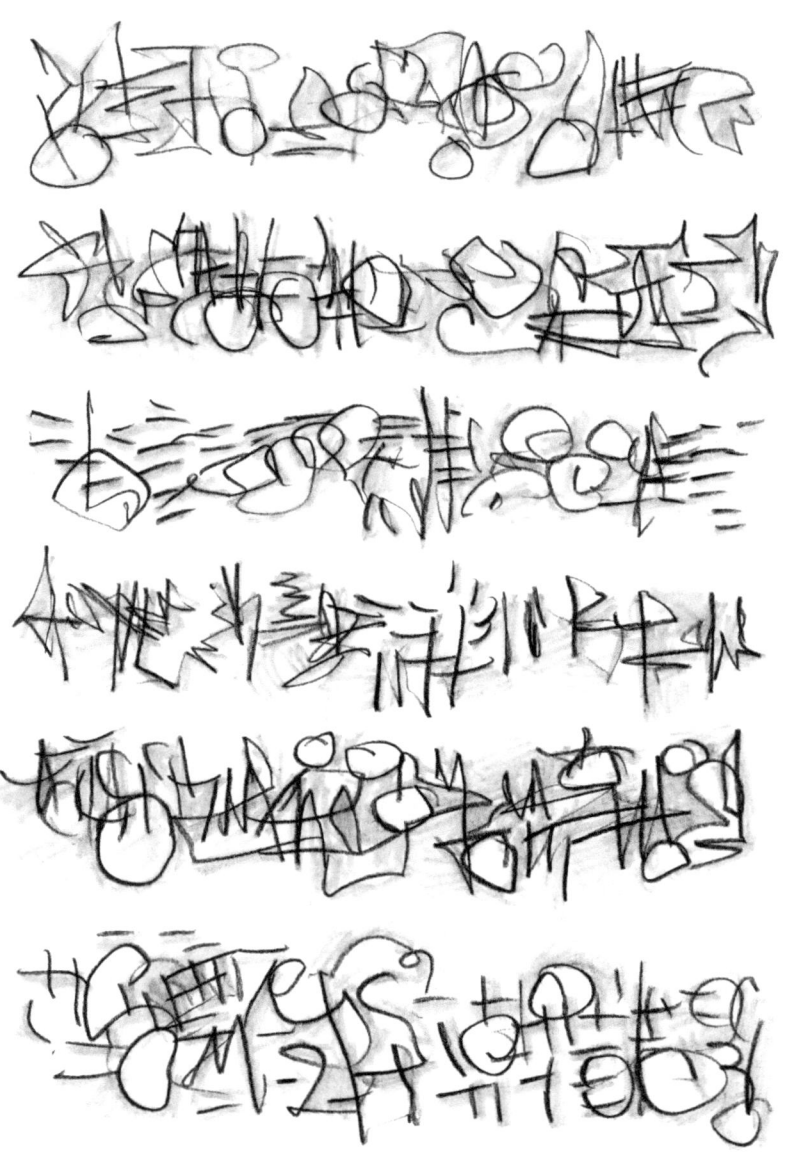

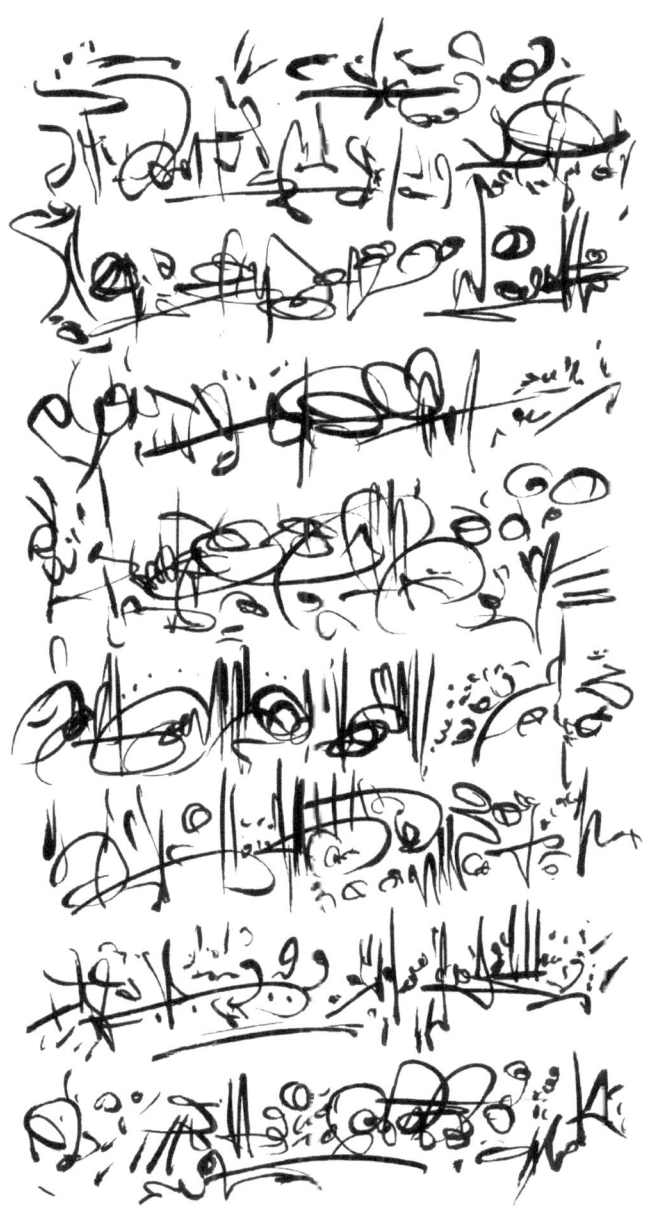

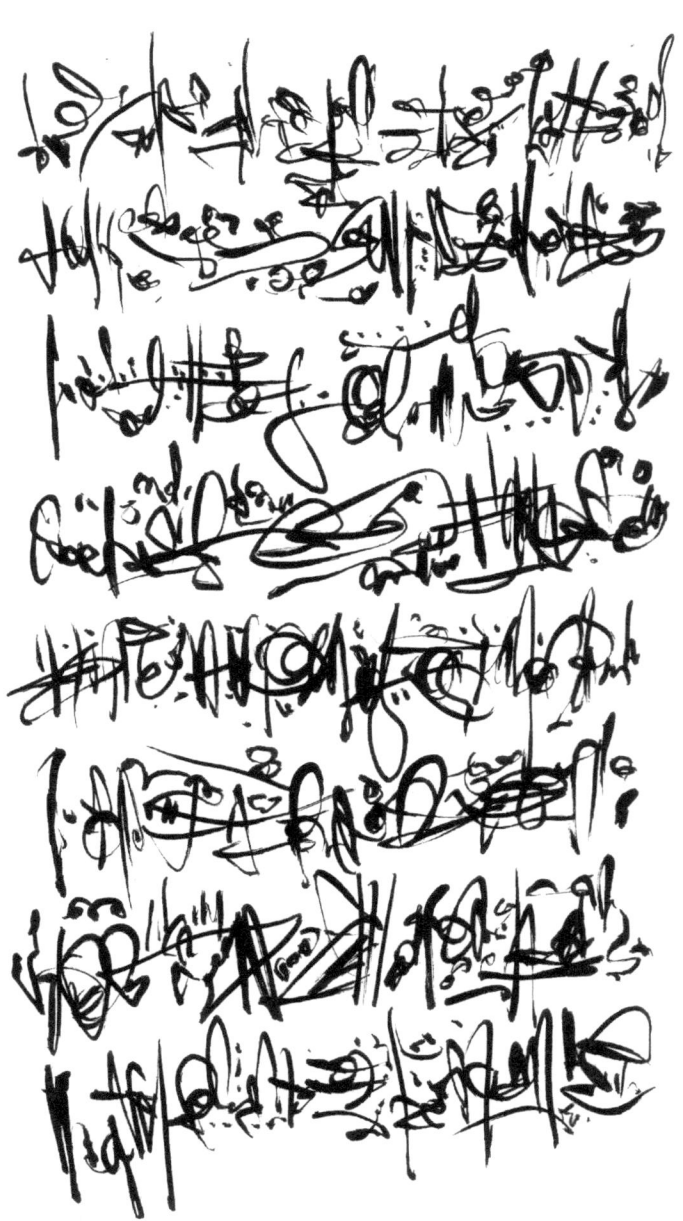

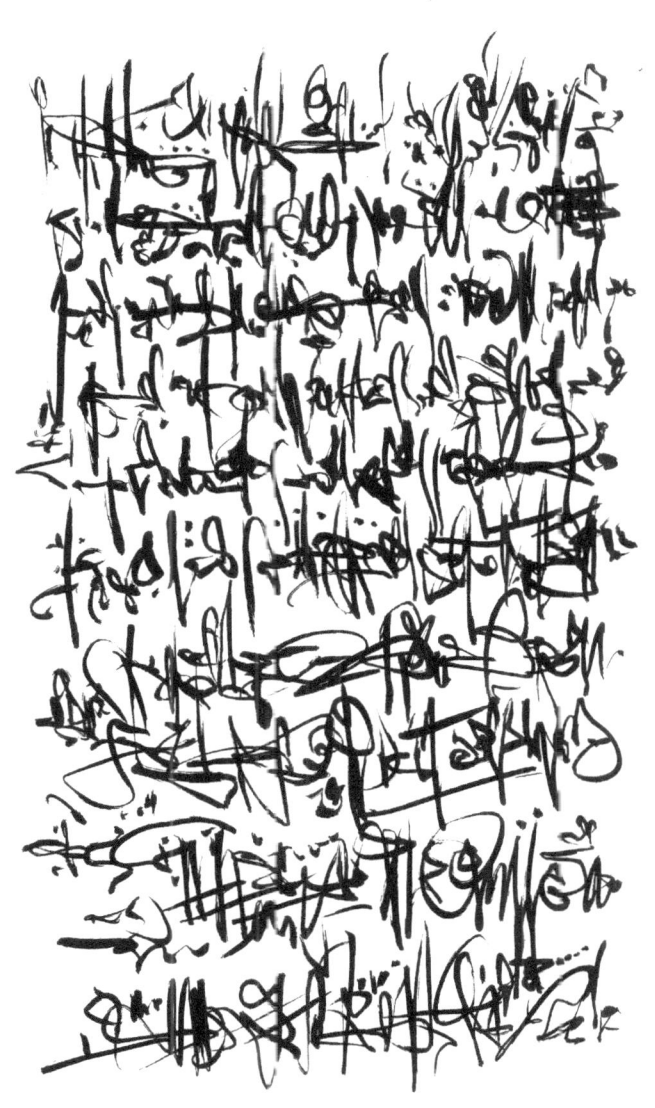

57. LIGHT OF FLAME.

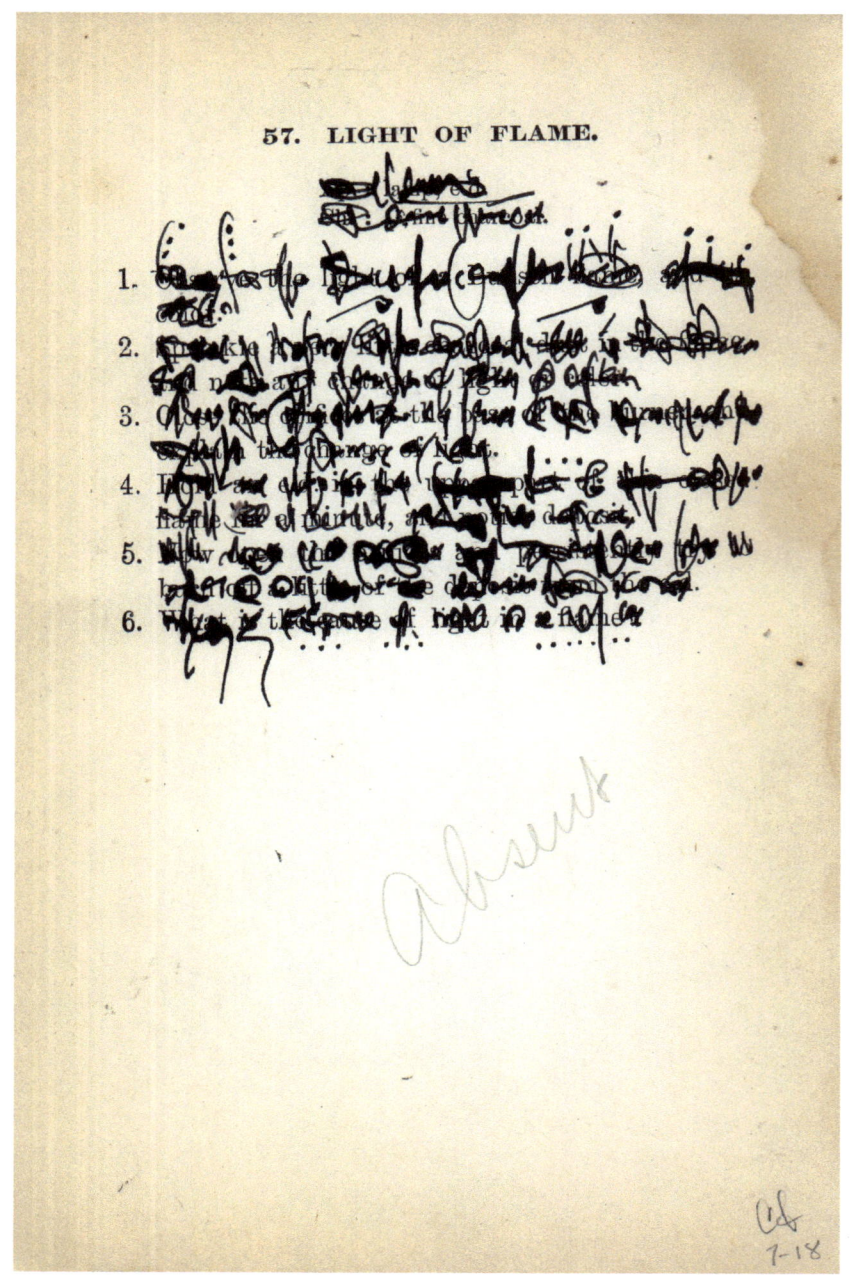

Tim Gaze
ASEMIC:
ASEMANTIC BUT NOT ASEMIOTIC

COMMENTS ON THE CUT-UP TECHNIQUE
January 2006

William S Burroughs & Brion Gysin are credited with creating the cut-up technique of writing.

After slicing though a pile of newspapers, Brion noticed that it was easy to juxtapose slices from different pages of newspaper, & create new, sometimes sensible texts. Essentially, a process of collage.

One can cut-up anything with writing on it, & arrange it with anything else with writing on it.

When these works have been published, they've often been reproduced in facsimile: the visual appearance of the arrangement is part of the composition.

Usually, these works are read as irrational or surprising texts. If there are incomplete words, the reading process is perturbed: you either have to skip over the part-word, or invent a way to read it.

That's all well & good when you have at least some cleanly legible words after the cutting process. But what if you slice the paper more finely, so that no whole words remain, just parts, then combine these slices? You get semi-words, some of them unpronounceable strings of letters.

Or what if you slice so finely that you cut the letters into pieces? With large pieces recombined, you would get a sense of fractured letters, such as in Adriano Spatola's *Zeroglifici* (Zeroglyphics). You might recognise the curves & stems of certain letters.

With really tiny pieces recombined, you would get a sense of noise. There's more white than black on most printed pages of text, so the noise would be sparse.

Another consideration is what angle you arrange each slice. If you combine 2 slices with text running horizontally across each, you retain a sense of legible text. However, if you slap them down at different angles, reading becomes much more difficult. You get something like tossed word salad.

Conjectures
July 2006

1) there's a deeper level of symbolic communication than written words

2) even fragments of symbols can be meaningful to the reader

art which uses words is coercive.

writing a word, one activates that word in a reader's mind. this is a form of mind control.

using open-ended, suggestive forms which are completed by the viewer or reader, it is possible to offer a less coercive experience. asemic writing & inkblot images are examples of suggestive forms.

we approach a piece of asemic writing like a child learning to read, or as an adult learning to read a new script such as Chinese.

book learning is little use in interpreting asemic writing. this is threatening to people who have a lot invested in book learning.

after many thousands of expeditions into the asemic domain, we humans will, no doubt, begin to map & understand it.[1]

---

1 In «QWERTY» #23, New Brunswick, Canada
Portuguese translation: «Confraria do Vento» #10, Rio de Janeiro, Brazil
http://www.confrariadovento.com/revista/numero10/ensaio01.htm
Russian translation: «SLOVA» #6, Smolensk, Russia
http://slova.name/slova-6/tim-geyz.html

THE CONTINUUM BETWEEN TEXT & IMAGE
May 2006

I have been working with the idea that there's a continuum extending from images to text. Where something sits on this continuum is subjective. One person sees a picture of a house (recognisable image); another sees a bundle of lines (abstract image). One person can read a piece of graffiti (legible writing); another can't (asemic writing). One person sees an unknown species of writing (asemic writing); another sees "spaghetti" (abstract image).

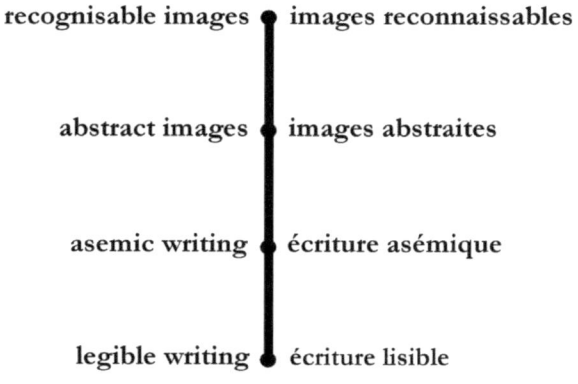

LE CONTINUUM ENTRE TEXTE & IMAGE
Juin 2008

J'avais travaillé avec l'idée qu'il y a un continuum s'étendant des images au texte. Se qui se pose à tel ou tel endroit du continuum est subjectif. Une personne voit l'image d'une maison (image reconnaissable); une autre voit un paquet de lignes (image abstraite). Une personne peut lire un morceau de graffiti (écriture lisible); une autre ne peut pas (écriture asémique). Une personne voit une espèce inconnue d'écriture (écriture asémique); une autre voit des «spaghettis» (image abstraite).[1]

---

[1] Version française de Damien Dion, éditée en «Toth» 1, Orléans, Déc. 2008

A FEW PERSISTENT THOUGHTS ABOUT ASEMIC WRITING
new version of essay originally published in «Utsanga» 04-2015

Asemic writing is a visual stimulus that makes one think, for however brief an amount of time, that one is looking at writing. Then, when you try to read it, you can't find any words.

I have a particular interest in asemic writing that is black and white, on paper, and to a large extent, reproduced rather than original.

Black and white are fundamental, and very powerful. A black and white form cannot be simplified, but can be dressed in any of a multitude of colours. A form rendered in only black and white can be considered to be a kind of template.

Paper is an ancient medium. According to legend, a Chinese eunuch named Cai Lun (蔡伦 Ts'ai Lun) invented paper. Certainly, paper was adopted first in China, then traded as far afield as Arabia, before finding its way to Europe. It is a more global medium than, for example, canvas, which is a relatively recent Western European invention.

If an original piece of writing is written in black ink on a white page, it can be reproduced with high fidelity. Minimal information is lost due to the reproduction process.

More fundamental than talking about asemic writing is to ask the question: *what is writing?*, which leads to the further question: *what is reading?*

Reading seems to operate at the level of habit. When legible words are placed in front of us, it's difficult and takes an effort of will not to begin reading those words.

Reading (or attempting to read) is a complex, multi-stage process, although we usually assume we're talking about a clearly legible text with sensible, easily comprehensible words. The very first stage is to recognise something as being readable. How long does this appraisal take? A fraction of a second.

An alternative definition for the English noun writing would be: any visual stimulus which activates the person viewing's reading habit.

Asemic writing can occur accidentally, such as when the wind and rain move sticks and other debris into shapes suggestive of letters or other symbols.

There are at least 3 broad approaches to deliberately making asemic writing:
• imitations of cursive handwriting;
• extending the repertoire of written symbols to include unknown ones;
• damaging the legibility of what would otherwise be legible writing.

Everybody is familiar with illegible or at least difficult-to-read cursive handwriting. The legendary Doctors' handwriting on prescriptions for medicine is an example. To create asemic handwriting, one can simply push to write more quickly than the hand can comfortably manage, and you'll skid off the road into asemic territory.

Chinese cursive is written vertically, from top to bottom in columns from right to left, rather than in horizontal lines from left to right. In ancient Egypt, a cursive script called demotic developed from the sheer difficulty of writing complex pictographic hieroglyphs. Cursive is fast, and can cover a lot of territory, both on the page and in terms of rapidity of capturing ideas.

The Belgian poet Christian Dotremont invented a method of writing asemic, pseudo-Mongolian writing: he wrote some French words in cursive on a translucent piece of paper, then rotated it and freely moved his brush over what he could see on the other side, writing downwards instead of across. Anyone can roughly imitate writing systems that they don't know. The results will probably look hilarious to someone who can fluently read that script.

There is a multitude of symbol systems beyond the written word. To mention a few: cattle brands, hobo signs, Bliss symbols, alchemical symbols, electrical circuit symbols, house decoration signs, Stonemasons' marks, tribal tattoos, even the separate traditions within prehistoric rock art. We can still create new symbols, although sometimes they are unintentionally similar to symbols which are already in use.

Creating one's own family of symbols, without a fixed meaning, is part of the Lettriste technique of hypergraphies, making compositions using elements beyond just the familiar letters and numbers. Finding your own symbols could be completely rational and cold-blooded, or it could be a personal spirit-quest.

Some symbols are so ubiquitous that we develop a numbness to them, and largely ignore them. The rectangle is a universal symbol which is deeply written into contemporary human culture. The shapes of screens (such as mobile phones and computer monitors) and the shape of a typical piece of paper imply a rectangle. This rectangle is present in every use of that medium. The rectangle is typical in books, 2-dimensional visual art, photographs, movies. It would be refreshing to encounter asemic writing which is framed in some way other than in a rectangle.

Unicode is an attempt to represent almost every extant writing system in the world in a standard digital format. Every one of the Unicode characters has been assigned a unique number or combination of numbers. ASCII was an earlier scheme to assign common characters used in English, along with a few from European languages, a unique numerical code.

Part of my attraction to asemic writing is that we can invent new characters, beyond even the 113,021 in the current version of Unicode. Thus, a scheme like Unicode can never represent all possible symbols.

When every symbol is mapped to a unique numerical code, the task of recognising letters is taken away from the reader. Recognising letters in a piece of writing is an early stage in attempting to read something. Characters represented in Unicode preclude the potential for enjoyable ambiguities or complete misreadings.

Another way to think about asemic writing is to consider information theory. The best-known assumption about passing information is that a message must be perfectly encoded. Misspelled words or missing words subtract from the total amount of information in the message. This is the mode of information which Unicode attempts to streamline.

Contrary to this, consider the message as being latent in the person receiving. The sender transmits a stimulus – a kind of rich noise – to the receiver, who decodes it according to her or his trained reading habits.

Pareidolia is a term for the human tendency to see concrete pictures in ambiguous shapes. People see animals or faces in clouds, and so on. An easier term would be *pattern-completion*. Because we have such a well-developed ability to perceive patterns, shapes such as inkblots or illegible calligraphy can stimulate one's mind to imagine what it thinks the missing details of the image might be.

There doesn't seem to be much research into pareidolia. Eventually, I suppose Cognitive Scientists will look into it. Cognitive poetics is a growing area, while cognitive approaches to art appreciation or image studies aren't as common.

The inkblot paintings by Victor Hugo and Henri Michaux are one step removed from asemic writing. Victor never tried his hand at asemic writing to the best of my knowledge, but Henri certainly did.

Elsewhere (such as *Asemic Movement* 1), I've published my idea that asemic writing sits on a continuum between legible writing and abstract images. Where something sits on this continuum is dependent on the person looking: one considers an example to be an abstract blob, while another can see a resemblance to writing but cannot read any words, hence it is asemic writing.

Damaging legible writing in order to render it illegible or only partly legible can be accomplished in a number of ways. If you begin with an object such as a page of written words, anything which physically alters that piece of paper has the potential to diminish the legibility. One could spray water at it, burn it, spray corrosive liquids at it, tear it, crumple it, punch holes in it, cut pieces off it. An old Chinese game was to place a piece of calligraphy into a container of water, which causes the ink to gently float out of the paper to form pleasing shapes in the water and the gradual disintegration of the original writing.

The designer of the music magazine Ray Gun, Dave Carson, often used typefaces which had slices taken out of the top or bottom or both. One interview was published in wingdings.

Collaging material with perfectly legible writing on it quickly tends towards producing asemic writing. So does glitching anything with text, such as when a digital television malfunctions while the credits are showing.

I'm throwing many ideas together here, unencumbered by academic style or references. I hope the train of my thoughts is digestible.

www.ingramcontent.com/pod-product-compliance
Lightning Source LLC
Chambersburg PA
CBHW040335220526
45473CB00009B/2694